GROWING UP
TOGETHER

In appreciation for your support of
Focus on the Family, please accept this
copy of *Growing Up Together,* by Jan
Kempe. Your contributions enable
this organization to address the needs
of homes through radio, television,
literature and counseling.

On the following pages you will find
simple and fun ideas for drawing
mom and child together while
teaching valuable biblical truths. We
trust that this handy resource will
make a fine addition to your home
library.

Focus on the Family
Pomona, CA 91799

Discovery House
PUBLISHERS
BOX 3566 · GRAND RAPIDS, MI 49501

*PUBLISHING BOOKS THAT FEED
THE SOUL WITH THE WORD OF GOD.*

Growing Up Together

Jan Kempe

Illustrations by **Nancy Munger**

TO my Lord, Jesus Christ, who is directly responsible for every good thing that happens in my life

TO my teachers—Krista, Kevin, Mikey, and Jon

TO Carol Holquist and Julie Ackerman Link and so many other talented people that God has used to help me

Thanks

GROWING UP TOGETHER

Copyright © 1989 by Jan Kempe

Discovery House Publishers is affiliated with Radio Bible Class, Grand Rapids, Michigan.

Designed by Rachel Hostetter

Produced by Blue Water Ink

Unless otherwise indicated, all Scripture quotations are from the *New International Version*. Copyright 1973, 1978, 1984 by the International Bible Society. Used by permission of Zondervan Bible Publishers.

Library of Congress Cataloging-in-Publication Data

Kempe, Janice.
    Growing up together : a special book for mom and child / Jan Kempe ; [illustrations by Nancy Munger].
        p.   cm.
    ISBN 0-929239-12-1
    1. Mothers—Prayer-books and devotions—English. 2. Children—Prayer-books and devotions—English. I. Munger, Nancy. II. Title.
BV4847.K46   1989
242'.6431—dc20   89-16955
                                                                              CIP
                                                                              AC

Printed in the United States of America

90 91 92 93 / CHG / 10 9 8 7 6 5 4 3

 CONTENTS

INTRODUCTION

"TRAIN A CHILD in the way he should go, and when he is old he will not turn from it" (Prov. 22:6).

As Christian moms our most important job is to show our children by our lives that being a Christian makes us special. They need to see us work at becoming more like Jesus. They need to hear us talk naturally about matters of faith and about how God helps us in the things we do each day. And they need to hear us pray.

With our busy, sometimes frantic, schedules, it is difficult to find time for our own spiritual health and growth.

Growing Up Together is a devotional journal and calendar to help us grow in our faith and, at the same time, to share the importance of our faith with our children. I am convinced that God will honor our efforts with insights that will enrich our relationship with Him and with our children.

The apostle Paul urges Christians to grow up in the faith (Eph. 4:14–15). What better way to grow up than in the company of our own children?

Growing Up Together is divided into twelve chapters, one for each month, and each chapter is divided into four weeks. Each month has a theme with a related meditation for mom, and each week has an activity for mom and one for mom and child.

The "Mom & Me" activity for week one of every month is something to hang up as a reminder of the topic for the month. Use this activity as a conversation piece with your child as you practice the weekly lessons. (Samples at the end of the book show you what the page should look like.) You may want to purchase an inexpensive calendar and paste your creations over the top half of the calendar each month. Doing so will give you a keepsake record of your year together in addition to this book. Also, since the book has twelve months of four weeks, it lacks four weeks of being a complete year. It will work fine as a devotional journal, but it might cause confusion if you try to use it as your yearly calendar.

The "Mom & Me" activities for weeks two and three will work best if you go over the lesson by yourself first. Some have a surprise, and a trial run will help you be sure to pull it off right with your child.

The "Mom & Me" activity for week four is a time to review the lesson you've learned together and read a story that illustrates it. Suggested readings are just that ... suggestions. Libraries and bookstores are filled with good books on these topics.

If you have more than one child, you can easily adapt the activities to suit your individual needs.

The materials needed for all activities are easy to find and inexpensive. Remember, the activities are meant to illustrate a lesson and won't necessarily look wonderful.

A memory verse for each month appears above the weekly calendars. You'll be surprised how easy memorization is when you have a child to help you.

Make the prayer list an important part of growing together. In the spaces provided, write specific concerns that you and your child have. Use the calendar space to note answers you receive. Our children need to see that prayer is much more than wishful thinking.

Immerse your child and these activities in prayer. I have been praying for you as I wrote the book. Surely God will bless you as you and your child grow up together to be more like our Lord Jesus.

May God bless you abundantly this year as you grow together.

Learning God's Word

JANUARY

I have hidden your word in my heart that I might not sin against you.

PSALM 119:11

JUST FOR MOM

M OMMY, WATCH THIS!"
     After drying my hands I moved over to see what four-year-old Kevin wanted to show me. He pointed to the page where he had printed his name for the first time. Some letters were capitals, some lower case, some faced backward, some leaned a bit too far left. But I could read KEVIN, and I was proud. We hung it on the refrigerator door and showed it to everyone who came by.
     "Mommy, watch this!"
     Three apples plus two more apples (painstakingly colored) equals five apples! Fantastic! A new master-piece adorns the refrigerator.
     "Mommy, do you know the names of the continents? Do you know that petroleum is the second largest industry in the American Southwest? Can I take flute and piano lessons? Can I join Cub Scouts?"
     The questions my children ask keep getting more difficult to answer, their accomplishments bigger. The day is not far off when my daughter's knowledge of some subjects will surpass mine. I thank God for the steps of learning He has allowed me to witness in my children. They are excited and hungry for more. I hope they never think they know enough to stop learning.
     I have saved samples of my children's lessons, and we have growth charts and baby books that herald the landmarks of development. Clearly, growth and maturation are essential in making a person.

I wish we could document our lives as Christians as easily. We celebrate such landmarks as baptism and joining a church, but some important steps of learning go unnoticed. When was the first time I recognized an answer to prayer? What about the first time I tried to witness, or the first time I tried to turn the other cheek? Have I grown? Has my understanding increased? Do I live more like Jesus than I did a few years ago?

In his letter to the Ephesians, Paul urged believers to grow up in their faith. All through his writings he encouraged new Christians to keep learning, growing, becoming. He prodded them to "walk worthy of God who calls you into His own kingdom and glory" (1 Thessalonians 2:12).

Seeing my children grow and develop physically and mentally reminds me that physical growth is not optional. Neither is spiritual growth. The only way to become spiritually healthy and mature is to grow to be more like Jesus each day.

LORD,

I have a long way to go. Show me how to help my family grow along with me this year.

ACTIVITIES

Week 1

Mom

Read 2 Peter 1:1–11. Peter knew Jesus well. He lived with Him for three years and was the center of many of the Lord's lessons and miracles. In this passage, Peter makes it clear that everything we want from this life is ours through the knowledge of God and our Lord Jesus (v. 3). Knowledge! This is a call to learn. Choosing not to learn is to miss out on wonderful things.

List the steps that lead from faith to love (vv. 5–7). Faith is only the beginning! We must grow before our lives exhibit Christ's love. Read verses 8–11 again. Is this how you choose to live?

Mom & Me

Tools: construction paper, crayons or markers.

1. With your child, draw a picture of how he or she may look some day. (See sample on page 152.)
2. At the bottom of the page write "I want to be ... " Think of as many positive adjectives as you can (e.g., brave, loving, kind, smart, happy) and list the ones your child agrees with at the bottom of the page.
3. **Explain:** *Jesus is all those things. He is strong and kind, brave and smart. Wouldn't it be good to grow up to be like Jesus?*
4. Add to your list "I want to be like Jesus."
5. **Explain:** *If we ask Him, Jesus will help us grow to be just like Him. When we learn about Jesus, love Him, and want to become like Him, we can ask Him into our hearts. We do this by telling Him we are sorry for the bad things we do and asking Him to forgive us and make us like Him.*
6. Tell your child how you became a Christian. If the Lord leads your child to a place of acceptance, pray with him and mark the day on the calendar with a sticker. Explain that all of heaven is celebrating because of his prayer (Luke 15:7–10).
7. Review the memory verse, fill in your prayer list, and pray together.

PSALM 119:11
I have hidden your word in my heart that I might not sin against you.

PRAY *EVERY* DAY
1.
2.
3.
4.

SUNDAY

MONDAY

TUESDAY

WEDNESDAY

THURSDAY

FRIDAY

SATURDAY

ACTIVITIES

Week 2

Mom

Read 2 Peter 1:12–21. Do you hear the urgency in Peter's voice? He is pointing to the proof of Jesus' Lordship and begging us to know it. We must know what the prophets foretold and be able to link those prophecies to the historical fulfillment in the life of Jesus.

Find five Old Testament prophecies that Jesus fulfilled. Read Psalm 22, written a thousand years before Jesus' birth, long before crucifixion was known. Compare verses 13–18 with what you know about Jesus' death.

Mom & Me

Tools: Bible, baby pictures of your child, a few things you saved from his infancy or early years.

1. Snuggle up in a cozy place and look at baby pictures and old things. Talk about what a special baby he was and about some of the firsts in his life—first steps, first words, etc. Tell him about the funny things he used to do.

2. Talk about your own childhood until he understands that you were a baby once and had to learn everything just the way he did. Tell him that even Grandma and Grandpa started out as babies and had to learn to sit up and walk and talk.

3. **Explain:** *People have to grow mentally and spiritually as well as physically. That's why we have schools and churches. We grow mentally by studying science, history, math, and English. We grow spiritually by studying the Bible and by praying. Jesus answers by helping us to think the right thoughts and to love one another.*

4. If you have a children's NIV Bible look at the picture of David by Psalm 91. **Explain:** *When David was a young boy he loved God. As he watched his father's sheep he sang songs about God and learned the things God had said. David became very strong. He became a great king. David grew strong in the Lord because he memorized God's Word. This week we will begin growing strong in the Lord as we memorize Psalm 119:11.*

(continued on page 156)

14

PSALM 119:11

*I have hidden your word in my
heart that I might not sin against
you.*

PRAY *EVERY* DAY
1.
2.
3.
4.

SUNDAY

MONDAY

TUESDAY

WEDNESDAY

THURSDAY

FRIDAY

SATURDAY

ACTIVITIES

Week 3

Mom

Read 2 Peter 2, a warning about false teachers. Christians today
need to increase their knowledge of truth so they can recognize
what isn't true. Not everyone who can afford time on radio or
television proclaims truth. Learn to be discerning. Ask "Where is
that written?" and never confuse modern opinion with biblical truth.
Are you familiar with the situation mentioned in verses 15–16? Read
Numbers 22–24, a strange and wonderful story.

Mom & Me

1. Visit someone you know who has a new baby, puppy, or kitten,
   or go to a zoo or farm where there are baby animals. If you can't
   get out, find a book with pictures of baby animals. Discuss some
   of the things the baby or the animals need to learn before they
   grow up.

2. **Explain:** *When we become Christians we say we are born again.
   We become babies in God's family. It is important for babies to
   learn and grow. If babies never grow, they just get to be big
   babies. We grow to be more like Jesus by learning about Him and
   by learning God's Word. We learn God's Word so we will know
   what is right and wrong, and so we will be able to choose what is
   right. Psalm 119:11 says, "I have hidden your word in my heart
   that I might not sin against you."*

3. Review the memory verse, update your prayer list, and pray
   together. Thank God that He wants to help us be more like Jesus.

PSALM 119:11
I have hidden your word in my heart that I might not sin against you.

PRAY *EVERY* **DAY**
1.
2.
3.
4.

SUNDAY

MONDAY

TUESDAY

WEDNESDAY

THURSDAY

FRIDAY

SATURDAY

ACTIVITIES

Week 4

Mom

Read 2 Peter 3. Peter learned many lessons the hard way. Toward the end of his life he understood the importance of learning and growing in the truth. In chapter 3 he pleads with Christians not to ignore this wonderful gift of truth, God's Word. He knew unbelievers would make fun. He had faced them and been persecuted by them. But he knew the way to stand firm in the faith and not be damaged by scoffers (v. 18). No surprise, is it?

Mom & Me

1. Suggested reading:
   Growing Strong Inside, Jennie Davis, Victor Books
   Jeremy, Barnabas and the Wonderful Dream, Joni Eareckson Tada, Chariot Books
   Tell Me About Jesus, Elizabeth Elaine Watson, Concordia Publishing House
2. Review the memory verse, update your prayer list, and pray together.

PSALM 119:11
I have hidden your word in my heart that I might not sin against you.

PRAY *EVERY* DAY
1.
2.
3.
4.

SUNDAY

MONDAY

TUESDAY

WEDNESDAY

THURSDAY

FRIDAY

SATURDAY

Learning To Be Kind

FEBRUARY

Be kind and compassionate to one another.

EPHESIANS 4:32

JUST FOR MOM

AND DON'T TOUCH my things again!"

What Kevin said didn't bother me as much as how he said it. I recognized my tone of voice coming from his six-year-old mouth as he scolded his little brother. How nasty it sounded! How unloving and unkind! I wish my kids had never heard me use that awful tone of voice. I wish I could stop sarcastic remarks or disapproving glances before they slip out. But too often I fail to do so.

Jesus was kind. Maybe I could become kinder by learning to think the way He thinks. Everything Jesus said or did passed through the wonderful love that God the Father has for His children. No wonder kindness came naturally to Jesus.

Perhaps the closest we can come to understanding God's love for His children is to compare it to our love for our own children. An unselfish, sometimes surprising love compels us to care for and protect our children. We rejoice in their accomplishments and ache when they hurt. Now think, *God's love for His children is far more powerful than the love I feel for my own children!*

As we try to become more like Jesus in our responses to people we need to keep three things in mind:

1. *God loves me more than I love my own children.* This awesome realization fills my mind with memories: of wishing I could take the fever for my sick little girl; of proudly displaying volumes of baby pictures to my friends; of tears that fill my eyes whenever I get one of

those precious, unsolicited hugs. And to think that God loves me more than that.

2. *God loves my children more than I do.* This shakes up my priorities some. A mom spends most of her waking hours organizing her children's schedules, anticipating their needs, and trying to provide the right balance of encouragement and discipline. I do my best, and turn to God in despair when I fail. How backward. That's like reading the recipe when the cake is in the oven. God knows what is best for my children, and my care of them would improve greatly if I could remember to consult Him first.

3. *God loves every person I meet more than I love my children.* Whether or not the people in my community love God is not the point. God loves them. He loves the pushy woman who slams her shopping cart into my ankle and the impatient man who blasts his horn when I don't move the second the traffic light turns green. They are as much the reason God sent Jesus as I am, and He cares how I treat them!

Why is it so hard to be kind? Why do I snap at those I love? When I think my own love is sufficient, I fail. Only when I am filled with the Father's love can I consistently treat others as He wants me to treat them.

Lord,

I want to be kind. Please make me like Jesus.

ACTIVITIES

Week 1

Mom

Write the following prayer on a 3 x 5 card and tape it to your bathroom mirror or refrigerator door, someplace where you will see it first thing each day: "Good morning, Lord! I know you love me more than anybody else does, and I thank you." Begin each day this week by taking a deep breath and saying the prayer aloud. This simple activity, which you can do even on the most frantic morning, will improve the start of your day if you do it thoughtfully and faithfully.

Mom & Me

Tools: large red construction paper heart, pen, scissors, magazines, glue, small picture of Jesus.

1. Draw a square in the center of the heart and leave it empty for now. (See sample on page 152.)
2. Have your child fill the rest of the heart with pictures of people she loves (pictures from magazines can be used instead of photographs to represent people she loves or she can draw the people).
3. Ask your child to name some of God's possessions that are special to her. **Explain:** *People are special to God because He made people more like Himself than anything else He created. God loves all the people He made: the ones we know and the ones we don't know; the ones we like and the ones we don't like; the ones who make us feel safe and the ones who make us feel afraid. Because we love God, it is important that we treat other people with care and respect.*
4. **Ask:** *Who do you think belongs in this special box in the center of your heart? Jesus does. When we have Jesus in our hearts and love Him more than anything, He gives us the love we need for everyone else. All God's people are special to Him, so let's look for ways to be kind this week. Does someone on our street need a special smile or visit? Is there someone at school who has nobody to play with and needs a kind friend? Each person we see is special to God.* (continued on page 156)

EPHESIANS 4:32
Be kind and compassionate
to one another.

PRAY *EVERY* DAY
1.
2.
3.
4.

SUNDAY

MONDAY

TUESDAY

WEDNESDAY

THURSDAY

FRIDAY

SATURDAY

ACTIVITIES

Week 2

Mom

To last week's prayer add, "I know that you love my kids more than anybody else does. Help me to treat them as you want me to treat them."

Yikes! Harsh words that previously slipped by unnoticed now remind you of your early morning prayer. Right the wrong and go on.

Mom & Me

Tools: construction paper, crayons or markers, old newspapers or magazines, family photo, paste.

1. Divide the page into three sections. Label the sections "My Favorite Things," "Mom's Favorite Things," and "God's Favorite Things."
2. Take turns drawing pictures of your favorite things in the appropriate boxes. While one draws the other can guess what it is.
3. When these two sections are complete, review the importance of respecting each other's property. Respecting things that are important to someone is one way to show we care about that person.
4. In the section marked "God's Favorites" put pictures of people. Draw them or cut them from old magazines or newspapers and paste them in the space. Include yourself, your child, and other family members. (A small photo would be ideal.) Include pictures of people who look different from you because of nationality or style of dress.
5. At the bottom of the page print "Because I love you I care about what is special to you." Read it together throughout the month to remind you that all God's children are special to Him and that because we love Him we will be kind to His children.
6. Any day this month that someone in the family goes out of the way to be kind to someone, mark the special day on the calendar with a smiley face (either hand-drawn or a sticker).
7. Review the memory verse, update your prayer list, and pray together.

EPHESIANS 4:32
Be kind and compassionate
to one another.

PRAY *EVERY* DAY
1.
2.
3.
4.

SUNDAY

MONDAY

TUESDAY

WEDNESDAY

THURSDAY

FRIDAY

SATURDAY

ACTIVITIES

Week 3

Mom

To your prayer add, "Everyone I meet today will be one of your children. I will treat them kindly because you love them."

Watch out! This week you may run into the most unlovable people you can imagine! Watch for them and go out of your way to smile or show respect. What an opportunity to practice kindness and to please the Father!

Mom & Me

Tools: Paper, markers or crayons, envelope.

1. Discuss what it means to be lonely. How does it feel? What would help?
2. Jesus said, "In everything, do to others what you would have them do to you" (Matt. 7:12). Make a greeting card for someone who is lonely. (Call your church office and get the name and address of someone who is confined to home or hospital due to illness or old age.)
3. Mail the card or make arrangements to deliver it in person.
4. Review the memory verse, update your prayer list, and pray together.

EPHESIANS 4:32
*Be kind and compassionate
to one another.*

PRAY *EVERY* DAY
1.
2.
3.
4.

SUNDAY

MONDAY

TUESDAY

WEDNESDAY

THURSDAY

FRIDAY

SATURDAY

ACTIVITIES

Week 4

Mom

This is a week for real challenge! To your previous prayer add these two dangerous sentences: "Someone needs to know about your love. Help me find that person and give him or her your message."

God will honor your request. Be ready. You may see one of God's children come to Him. Then all heaven will rejoice! This is powerful stuff.

Mom & Me

1. Suggested reading:
    Luke 10:29–37
    Let's Talk About Being Selfish, Joy Wilt Berry, Children's Press
    Shadow Chaser, Stephen Cosgrove, Multnomah Press
    Kiri and the First Easter, Carol Greene, Concordia Press (Arch Books)
    The Kindness Weapon, Bruce Wannamaker, Victor Books
    The Giving Tree, Shel Silverstein, Harper & Row
2. Review the memory verse, update your prayer list, and pray together.

EPHESIANS 4:32
*Be kind and compassionate
to one another.*

PRAY *EVERY* DAY
1.
2.
3.
4.

SUNDAY

MONDAY

TUESDAY

WEDNESDAY

THURSDAY

FRIDAY

SATURDAY

Learning To Be Patient

MARCH

But the fruit of the Spirit is love, joy, peace, patience, kindness, goodness, faithfulness, gentleness, and self-control. Against such things there is no law.

GALATIANS 5:22–23

❀ JUST FOR MOM ❀

THE CHILDREN were still asleep. Jon was away on business. The house remained peaceful while I had my devotions. As I finished praying for the things on my list, my mind turned to a discipline I needed in my own life. "Lord, please give me patience with my kids," I added.

When the kids tumbled out of bed and found their way to the kitchen, I greeted them with a smile. But I got none in return. I didn't even get a good morning greeting before I had to settle the day's first dispute. They were not in a good mood. The cereal had crumbs in it, the milk spilled, the toast burned, and the right clothes were not clean for gym day. By the time I got them on the bus I was ready for Mikey's nap, but Mikey wasn't.

There was no good mail. I got three calls from people trying to sell me things I didn't want, and each call came when I was at the other end of the house from the phone and had to run upstairs to answer. The drain in my laundry tub swallowed a rag, and the washer emptied onto all the clean clothes piled neatly by the machine. I washed my favorite angora sweater by mistake and it smelled like a dog ... a very little dog!

Supper looked promising until Michael got sick in the kitchen. Nobody felt much like eating after that. By the time I fished the toothbrushes out of the drain (thank you, Kevin) and got the kids into bed I was ready for bed myself. I decided I needed therapy more than sleep, however, so I called my sister. The conversation began

with small talk, but soon I was into heavy-duty complaining. I knew she would understand. "Never pray for patience," she said. "When you do, the Lord will give you plenty of chances to develop it."

The next morning I again finished my devotions with prayer, but I delayed asking for what I needed but didn't want to learn. When I could put it off no longer, I added, very quickly and in a small voice, "Oh yes, and I could use a bit more patience with my kids. Amen!"

Talk about fast answers to prayer! Breakfast turned into a disaster. Milk spilled, sugar spilled, the bananas were black, and the dog ate the toast. But this time I knew what was happening. "Oh no you don't," I said. "With God's help I can overcome this."

To say my day was a complete success would be a lie, but it wasn't a total failure either. Aware that exercises in patience were filling my day, I changed my attitude. I could become more patient, but it would take work. The devil might increase the level of difficulty, but never beyond God's capability in me!

Only with resistance can we build muscles. Only by challenging the limits can we set new records. Only by facing the enemy can we defeat him, and only by defeating him can we become more like Jesus.

LORD,

>   *I feel great! I had a lousy day, but
> I think we won!*

ACTIVITIES

Week 1

Mom

Read Galatians 5:22–23, which lists the fruits of the Spirit. Patience falls right in the middle of the list. In the life of a Spirit-filled Christian, patience is not an option.

Pray for patience every morning this week. Keep a diary of each day's events that help you learn patience. Record how well you did on each lesson.

Mom & Me

Tools: construction paper, pen or pencil, crayons or markers.

1. Draw a picture of a butterfly on the construction paper. (See the sample on page 152.) Use the chart below to find out what colors to use.
   1. yellow
   2. red
   3. blue
   4. purple
   5. green
   6. black

2. Discuss patience. **Explain:** *We are being patient when we work on something or wait for something without getting upset or giving up. We will be learning about patience this month. Butterflies must be patient to get out of their cocoons, and you need patience to color this picture. Each time one of us is patient this month, let's mark that special day on the calendar with a butterfly picture or sticker.*

3. Review the memory verse, update your prayer list, and pray together. Emphasize patience.

GALATIANS 5:22–23

But the fruit of the Spirit is love, joy, peace, patience, kindness, goodness, faithfulness, gentleness, and self-control. Against such things there is no law.

PRAY *EVERY* **DAY**

1.
2.
3.
4.

SUNDAY

MONDAY

TUESDAY

WEDNESDAY

THURSDAY

FRIDAY

SATURDAY

ACTIVITIES

Week 2

Mom

If you were honest last week, you will be able to look at your diary
and find one situation that really tested your patience (e.g., when
the kids fought over who got to sit by the window in the car). Make
your morning prayer more specific this week. Ask the Lord to help
you develop patience in that specific situation. Then work on it
whenever the opportunity arises. Continue your diary.

Mom & Me

Tools: a picture of a butterfly (hand-drawn or cut from a magazine,
brightly colored, at least 4 inches long), an empty toilet paper roll,
tape, scissors, brown paper, green paper, toilet paper.

    Advance preparation: Cut out the butterfly picture. Roll it gently
and put it inside the toilet paper roll. Wrap the roll with brown
paper, making sure both ends are covered. The children must not
know about the butterfly inside.

1. Discuss the meaning of patience with your child. **Explain:**
    *Patience means waiting or working on something without getting
    upset or giving up.* Ask him to think of a time when he acted
    patiently.
2. Give him the green paper and scissors and have him cut out a
    green caterpillar. **Explain:** *Caterpillars know how to do three
    things: crawl around, eat a lot of leaves (use your cutout to act
    this out), and make a special sleeping bag. God put those three
    directions into the mind of every caterpillar. We call it instinct
    when God's animals know what to do.*
3. Pretend the toilet paper roll is a tree branch. Have your child
    make the caterpillar crawl onto the roll. Use a piece of tape to
    hold him to the outside of the roll. Use the toilet paper to make
    his sleeping bag. Very gently wrap the paper around the whole
    thing. Wrap until the caterpillar is covered by the sleeping bag
    around him. (Make sure the end of the roll remains accessible so
    you can pull out the hidden butterfly later!)
4. **Explain:** *The caterpillar must be patient while God makes his
    work into something special. He waits and waits until he knows it
    is time to work again.*

(continued on page 156)

GALATIANS 5:22–23

But the fruit of the Spirit is love, joy, peace, patience, kindness, goodness, faithfulness, gentleness, and self-control. Against such things there is no law.

PRAY *EVERY* DAY

1.
2.
3.
4.

SUNDAY

MONDAY

TUESDAY

WEDNESDAY

THURSDAY

FRIDAY

SATURDAY

ACTIVITIES

Week 3

Mom

Read 1 Peter 2:20–21. The New American Standard Version says we are to endure with patience. When we are stressed to the limit and have to put up with other people's cruelty or intolerance, we are to endure it with patience. No temper tantrums, no speeches. We are to follow Christ's example.

This week someone may inconvenience you or take advantage of you. One of your children might thoughtlessly disobey. Or the person who always goes on and on about her troubles may call at your busiest time of the day. If so, endure with patience. How do you do that? Read Psalm 40:1–3, take a deep breath, and wait.

Mom & Me

1. Plan an outing with your child to run errands.
2. **Explain:** *Sometimes when I run errands I get impatient because I have to wait in long lines or I get caught in slow traffic. But Jesus doesn't want us to lose our tempers. He never had tantrums or stamped His feet and demanded, "Me first." He was patient, and He wants to help us be patient. Today on our outing we are going to help each other practice patience. Every time you see me being patient, give me this secret sign (show thumbs up), and I will do the same for you. If we are patient for the whole trip we will have a special reward.* (Decide ahead of time what the reward will be.)
3. Review the memory verse, update your prayer list, and pray together for patience.

GALATIANS 5:22–23

But the fruit of the Spirit is love, joy, peace, patience, kindness, goodness, faithfulness, gentleness, and self-control. Against such things there is no law.

PRAY *EVERY* DAY

1.
2.
3.
4.

SUNDAY

MONDAY

TUESDAY

WEDNESDAY

THURSDAY

FRIDAY

SATURDAY

❊ ACTIVITIES ❊

Week 4

Mom

Read Psalm 37:7–11. In these days of uncertain social values, political corruption, and confused morality, it is easy for Christians to despair. But we can take strength and peace from David's words and remember that although the devil seems to be making significant strides in this world, one day evil will be put in its place. If we are faithful and wait patiently, the Lord will work out His will for our lives.

Watch the news this week for examples of God's people overcoming Satan by exercising patience. If you find one, drop the person a note of encouragement and appreciation for the evidence of patience in his or her action.

Mom & Me

1. Try to find a cassette or record of "The Music Machine." (You can buy one from a Christian bookstore or borrow one from a friend or your church library.) Play the song about Herbert, the snail, and enjoy it with your child.
2. Suggested Reading:
    Let's Talk About Throwing Tantrums, Joy Wilt Berry, Children's Press
    The Very Hungry Caterpillar, Eric Carle, Putnam
    Barney Wigglesworth and the Birthday Surprise, Elspeth Campbell Murphy, Chariot Books
3. Review the memory verse, update your prayer list, and pray together.

GALATIANS 5:22–23

*But the fruit of the Spirit is love, joy,
peace, patience, kindness, goodness,
faithfulness, gentleness, and self-control.
Against such things there is no law.*

PRAY *EVERY* DAY

1.
2.
3.
4.

SUNDAY

MONDAY

TUESDAY

WEDNESDAY

THURSDAY

FRIDAY

SATURDAY

Learning
To
Forgive

APRIL

Bear with each other and forgive whatever grievances you may have against one another. Forgive as the Lord forgave you.

COLOSSIANS 3:13

JUST FOR MOM

KEVIN WAS EAGER for a second piece of warm banana bread. He moved close to the breadboard to supervise me as I sliced another steamy piece.

"Wow, Mom! You almost cut my eye out!" he yelled, jerking his head away from the counter. Having his face at breadboard level apparently made that big knife seem too close, even though it was a safe distance from him.

"I'm sorry," I replied.

"That's okay, Mom. You're forgiven. Do you know what forgiven means, Mom? It means forgot. Forgiven means that I forgot all about it that you almost cut my eye out with that big knife."

"Thanks, Kev," I replied as I went back to fixing lunch.

"You see," he continued, "if I say you're forgiven I really mean that I forgot about what you did when you almost cut my eye out. It means that I don't even remember it anymore and that's why I said you're forgiven."

After bestowing bushels of forgiveness on his unworthy mother, Kevin finally left the room with his banana bread. In a few moments he returned.

"Mom? Can I have just one more little piece?"

I consented and headed back to the breadboard.

"Now be careful so you don't cut my eye out this time! Remember what I said before when I said you were forgiven and then I forgot?"

My son's knowledge of forgiveness was incomplete. Knowing what forgiveness is and knowing how to forgive are two very different things. Is this the example I give to my children? Do I say I forgive them for their shortcomings and then remind them of every mistake they've made? In my eagerness to use my kids' mistakes as teaching tools do I end up teaching them that they are never really forgiven?

Praise God that He doesn't deal with us that way. When I bring my sins to Him and ask for forgiveness, those sins are GONE!

LORD,

I need to be more forgiving. Each time I pray, "...and forgive us our debts as we forgive our debtors," help me remember that forgiving is forgetting!

ACTIVITIES

Week 1

Mom

Before we can practice forgiving we need to be forgiven. Make a list of things that need to be removed from your life (bad habits, impure thoughts, weaknesses). Read Psalm 139:23–24. Take the list before the Lord and ask for forgiveness. Experience God's forgiveness and enjoy a fresh start. Destroy the list.

Mom & Me

Tools: Construction paper, crayons or markers.

The activity page this month is a lovely garden ... well almost! It will be lovely when you finish it.

1. On the activity page this month draw stems and leaves. (See sample on page 153). Have your child use the brightest colors you have to make flowers on the stems. (For a little diversity, mom, don't be afraid to let her use poster paint.)
2. **Explain:** *A life filled with things that please the Lord is like a beautiful garden. Sin is like ugly weeds that grow up and kill the flowers. Let's try to keep our lives free of weeds this month.*
3. Help your child think of times when sin (lying, cheating, losing her temper) destroyed some good things in her life.
4. **Explain:** *When we ask God to forgive our sins, He pulls up those ugly old weeds so flowers can grow again.*
5. **Explain:** *God expects us to forgive others just as He forgives us. Forgiving our friends and families when they do things that hurt us is a good way to keep ugly weeds from messing up our friendships and our homes.*
6. Print this month's memory verse at the bottom of the garden. Say it every morning at breakfast and soon you will know it by heart.
7. Any time you or one of your children has a special experience with forgiveness this month, celebrate it together by marking the special day on your calendar with a picture of a flower or a flower sticker.
8. Review the memory verse, update your prayer list, and pray together.

COLOSSIANS 3:13

Bear with each other and forgive
whatever grievances you may
have against one another. Forgive
as the Lord forgave you.

PRAY *EVERY* DAY
1.
2.
3.
4.

SUNDAY

MONDAY

TUESDAY

WEDNESDAY

THURSDAY

FRIDAY

SATURDAY

ACTIVITIES

Week 2

Mom

This week your little angel may draw a masterpiece on your new wallpaper or flush her socks down the commode. This will be your opportunity to practice what you are trying to teach. Reprimand her firmly, but gently. Punish her appropriately, and make sure you hear her say "I'm sorry." Give her a hug. Tell her she is forgiven. And NEVER mention the act again.

Mom & Me

Tools: paper, pencil, transparent tape, toothpicks, a bowl, water, pepper, liquid dish detergent.

1. Ask your child to explain what God's will means to her.
2. On a small piece of paper write "God's will." Trim it to fit under a piece of tape. Tape it to the inside bottom of the bowl, making sure the tape completely covers the paper. Fill the bowl three-quarters full of water. (You should be able to read "God's will" through the water.)
3. Ask your child if the water is clean or dirty. Discuss some characteristics of clean water (e.g., there is nothing floating in it, you can see through it, etc.).
4. **Explain:** *The clean water is a picture of the way God wants our hearts to be. When we look into our hearts we see God's will clearly.*
5. Shake a little pepper into your hand. **Explain:** *Each dark speck represents sin, something we do that displeases God.*
6. Ask your child to name some of those things.
7. Shake some pepper gently on top of the water. Do not stir the water or break the surface tension. Ask your child if she can still see God's will clearly.
8. **Explain:** *Sin hides God's will from us. If our lives become filled with sin, we cannot know what God wants us to do.*
9. With a toothpick try to pick up some bits of pepper. Be careful not to stir up the water or cause too many bits to sink. **Say:** *Maybe I can clean up my life if I work at it really hard!* When your child senses the futility, **ask:** *Do you think I can make my heart clean by working at it really hard like this?*

(continued on page 156)

COLOSSIANS 3:13

Bear with each other and forgive
whatever grievances you may
have against one another. Forgive
as the Lord forgave you.

PRAY *EVERY* DAY

1.
2.
3.
4.

SUNDAY

MONDAY

TUESDAY

WEDNESDAY

THURSDAY

FRIDAY

SATURDAY

ACTIVITIES

Week 3

Mom

It's hard to forgive someone who doesn't ask to be forgiven. It's hard to be a Christian when a stranger is rude or takes advantage of us. This week watch for opportunities to forgive people you feel don't deserve it. When you receive a nasty gesture from someone, return a kind smile. Allow an impatient person to get in line in front of you. Let your light shine so that others will see your good deeds and praise your Father in heaven (Matt. 5:16).

Mom & Me

1. Ask your child to show you how big God is. **Explain:** *Today we are going to find out what the Bible says about how big God's love is. We will also learn how big His forgiveness is.*
2. Take your child to a pretty place with a good view (e.g., a hilltop or the top of a building).
3. Read Psalm 103:11. Talk about how high the heavens are above the earth.
4. Read Psalm 103:12. Discuss how far you can see to the east and west. **Explain:** *If you went east and I went west until we were as far apart as possible, that's how big God's forgiveness is. He takes our sin as far away as possible.*
5. Review the memory verse, update your prayer list, and pray together.

COLOSSIANS 3:13

*Bear with each other and forgive
whatever grievances you may
have against one another. Forgive
as the Lord forgave you.*

PRAY *EVERY* DAY

1.
2.
3.
4.

SUNDAY

MONDAY

TUESDAY

WEDNESDAY

THURSDAY

FRIDAY

SATURDAY

ACTIVITIES

Week 4

Mom

Read Matthew 5:23–24. Whom have you offended? Perhaps someone has been mad at you for years and it isn't even your fault. Now is the time to go to the person and ask to be reconciled. (Cover your actions in prayer *first*.)

Mom & Me

1. Read Luke 15:11–24 together. Assure your children that they will always be loved in your home, and that God will always love them too.
2. Suggested reading:
    Spotlight on Charity, Ken Gire, Focus on the Family
    A Picnic with the Barleys, Karen Mezek, Harvest House
    God Cares When Somebody Hurts Me, Elspeth Campbell Murphy, Chariot Books
    Sometimes It's Hard to be Friends, Elspeth Campbell Murphy, Chariot Books
    The Adventures of Andy Ant—Lawn Mower on the Loose, Gerald P. O'Nan, Tyndale
    Andy Ant—the Band Music Mystery, Gerald P. O'Nan, Tyndale
3. Review the memory verse, update your prayer list, and pray together.

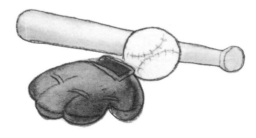

COLOSSIANS 3:13

Bear with each other and forgive
whatever grievances you may
have against one another. Forgive
as the Lord forgave you.

PRAY *EVERY* DAY

1.
2.
3.
4.

SUNDAY

MONDAY

TUESDAY

WEDNESDAY

THURSDAY

FRIDAY

SATURDAY

Learning
To
Praise

MAY

*I will extol the Lord at all times;
his praise will always be on my
lips.* PSALM 34:1

♪ JUST FOR MOM ♪

WHO CAN TELL ME what praise means?" I asked my new Sunday school class of about 60 children.

After a lively discussion we concluded that praise is saying (or singing) something good about someone and that it is a good thing to do, especially in church.

"So, now I need a volunteer. I would like to praise somebody."

Hands shot up all over. I selected a well-liked fourth grade boy who jumped to his feet.

"Listen carefully while I praise—uh, what's your name?"

"David."

"Listen carefully while I praise David. David is a wonderful boy." He smiled broadly. "He is so well-mannered." David flexed his muscles and grinned. "And you should see him play hockey!" David's grin faded. "You know he won the Stanley Cup all by himself last year as the youngest professional hockey player ever." The children, including David, began to giggle. "This incredible boy is so talented that he even sewed his own uniform."

"Hey," David tried to interrupt.

"And right after church today he is going to buy us all ice cream."

"I did not say that," David yelled, "and I don't sew."

"Wait a minute," I said to the children, "what's wrong? I'm saying nice things about David, and I'm in

church. Would it be better if I sang his praises?"

"You can't praise me like that because you don't know anything about me!" David replied.

"You mean you don't enjoy my praise when I don't know what I'm talking about? Hmm. That's interesting. Let's talk about the way we praise God."

This lesson in praise made such an impression on me and the children that we worked all that fall on getting to know God and His promises so that we could give Him meaningful praise.

Praise offered out of personal experience and knowledge is what God wants from us. And the more we investigate what He has done and who He is, the easier our praise will flow.

Praise does not depend on our mood (Acts 16:16–33). When our situation is oppressive we can think of the faithfulness of God and break into praise. I am convinced that praise offered in such times will not only bless God but will profoundly change our own attitude.

Just think, our praise actually blesses God (Psalm 34:1).

LORD,

Thank you for the privilege of praising you.

 **ACTIVITIES**

Week 1

Mom

Find a record or cassette of good Christian music. Play it at least twice each day. Listen for lyrics from Scripture. Learn the words and sing along. It doesn't matter whether or not you can carry a tune. If you are inhibited, sing while you run the vacuum or some other noisy appliance. Ask the Lord to accept your praise and to give you a spirit of praise. Anticipate a week of blessings. Continue this throughout the month, or longer.

Mom & Me

Tools: construction paper, pen or pencil, crayons or markers. Follow the steps below and write a psalm of praise to God to decorate this month's activity page. (See page 153.)

1. To give praise we must know what we are talking about. With your child, think of things God has done that you are grateful for (e.g., He made us, He made animals, He sent Jesus, He makes sunshine). Choose one. This will be the name of your psalm.
2. Psalms are written to God, so start your psalm by addressing the Lord (Dear God, Dear Father, Oh God, etc.).
3. Write a few lines that state simply what God has done that you think is so neat. Be descriptive.
4. Tell God about your love for Him and mention the ways you will praise Him (e.g., I will sing songs about you, I will learn about you, I will say your name when I am afraid).
5. Help your child to copy the psalm onto the construction paper (or copy it yourself). Then have him decorate the page. Don't forget to put the authors' names on it.
6. Review the memory verse, update your prayer list, and pray together. Emphasize praise.

PSALM 34:1
I will extol the Lord at all times;
his praise will always be on my
lips.

PRAY *EVERY* **DAY**
1.
2.
3.
4.

SUNDAY

MONDAY

TUESDAY

WEDNESDAY

THURSDAY

FRIDAY

SATURDAY

ACTIVITIES

Week 2

Mom

Read a Psalm each day. The following Psalms were written in all sorts of circumstances: Psalm 23, 24, 25, 27, 32, 34, 40, 48, 66, 69.

Mom & Me

Tools: Bible (preferably one written in easy-to-understand English), waxed paper and a comb (to use as a homemade kazoo), spoons (to clack together against your knee or thigh), kazoos, a musical instrument if someone in the family plays one, or any other good noise maker.

1. **Explain:** *Praise is showing or telling somebody what we think about the good things they have done. We can praise by using words, music, or dancing.* Discuss with your child the meaning and methods of praise and tell him about David the shepherd who became David the king.

2. **Explain:** *King David in the Old Testament didn't become a great king overnight. He first became a great man. By spending a lot of time with God, he got to know God very well. When David was just a little boy he took care of his dad's sheep. People back then didn't have Walkmans or books like ours for entertainment, so David took his harp and spent his free time making up songs. He loved God very much, so many of his songs were about the wonderful things God had done. David's songs are called Psalms of praise. David grew to be strong in the Lord because he praised God every day. If we praise God every day, we will grow strong in the Lord like David.*

3. Read one of David's Psalms to your child (23 and 100 are short and easy to understand).

4. Sing praise songs with your child. ("Jesus Loves Me," "Praise Him, Praise Him," "This Little Light of Mine," "God is so Good," "Heavenly Sunshine," and "Jesus Loves the Little Children" are good praise songs.) Pass out the noise makers. Have fun with this. Improvise and think of new ways to tell God you love Him.

5. Review the memory verse, update your prayer list, and pray together.

PSALM 34:1
I will extol the Lord at all times;
his praise will always be on my
lips.

PRAY *EVERY* DAY
1.
2.
3.
4.

SUNDAY

MONDAY

TUESDAY

WEDNESDAY

THURSDAY

FRIDAY

SATURDAY

ACTIVITIES

Week 3

Mom

Look for ways to praise the Lord when things aren't going well this week. Praise must be genuine, so avoid spreading flippant "Praise the Lord" comments. When something unfortunate happens, take your example from King David who honestly brought his problems before the Lord, got everything into the open, and then looked at the situation one more time to see where God's protective hand had been during the difficulty. Funny thing ... it was always there!

Mom & Me

Tools: paper, crayons or markers, pen or pencil.

1. With your child, think of a relative or friend (maybe a Sunday school teacher) who loves the Lord and deserves praise for being a special person.
2. Make a list of the special qualities God has put inside that person (e.g., kindness, a loving smile, good ideas).
3. Make your list into a short letter. Begin like this: "I am praising God today because He made you."
4. Fold your paper like a greeting card and decorate it.
5. Print your letter inside the card.
6. Mail it today.
7. Review the memory verse, update your prayer list, and pray together.

PSALM 34:1
I will extol the Lord at all times;
his praise will always be on my
lips.

PRAY *EVERY* DAY
1.
2.
3.
4.

SUNDAY

MONDAY

TUESDAY

WEDNESDAY

THURSDAY

FRIDAY

SATURDAY

ACTIVITIES

Week 4

Mom

Compose your own psalm of praise this week. If it is very personal you may want to keep it in your diary or Bible, or it may be so beautiful that you'll want to make it into a cross-stitch wall hanging. It is a privilege to praise God. Enjoy it!

Mom & Me

1. Pray with your child near a window or outside with your eyes open. Praise God for the sun, clouds, ladybugs, leaves ... everything you see!

2. Suggested reading:

    Everybody Shout Hallelujah! Elspeth Campbell Murphy, Chariot Books

    Make Way for the King, Elspeth Campbell Murphy, Chariot Books

    Come Sing God's Song, Thomas Paul Thigpen, Chariot Books

    All God's Critters Got a Place in the Choir, Bill Staines, E. P. Dutton

3. Review the memory verse, update your prayer list, and pray together.

PSALM 34:1
I will extol the Lord at all times;
his praise will always be on my
lips.

PRAY *EVERY* DAY
1.
2.
3.
4.

SUNDAY

MONDAY

TUESDAY

WEDNESDAY

THURSDAY

FRIDAY

SATURDAY

Following God's Directions

JUNE

In the same way, let your light shine before men, that they may see your good deeds and praise your Father in heaven.

MATTHEW 5:16

⭐ JUST FOR MOM ⭐

T HE NEW GAS GRILL we bought looked great in the store, and Jon and I felt pleased with our purchase as we lugged it home. But when Jon opened the huge box there was no gas grill inside. Instead he found hundreds of screws, washers, pieces of metal, tanks, an assortment of other strange objects, and a book of directions. I laughed a rather nervous laugh and excused myself from the scene. Jon, however, opened the book and began laying the pieces in neat piles. It took him about three hours, but we grilled our supper that night on a perfectly assembled gas grill.

I'm not much for directions. I push all of the Christmas presents that require assembly toward my very patient husband. Something in my nature longs for creativity and freedom to experiment. I don't like being told by any person (or piece of paper) how to do something. Consequently, I rarely get all of the pieces to fit into any mechanical gizmo.

Our life in Christ is a relationship and a discipline that requires careful attention to the book of directions. Creativity and freedom fit well into a Christian lifestyle, but only inside the framework of Scripture. When we neglect to follow the directions given there, the pieces don't fit together in the way God intended.

Naaman, an Old Testament ruler, had leprosy, a disease as frightening then as AIDS is now. Elisha responded to his request for help with some very strange directions: Go wash in the Jordan seven times.

Hardly sound medical advice. Yet Naaman followed the directions exactly, and he was healed (2 Kings 5:10).

To heal a blind man Jesus spit in the dirt, smeared the mud on the man's eyes, then told him to wash the mud off in the pool of Siloam. The man could have rubbed the stuff off onto his shirt, but he followed the directions and gained his sight (John 9:7).

Another man had been lame for years. He might have laughed when Jesus told him to stand and pick up his bed, but he followed the directions and walked home (Matthew 9:6–7).

There are directions for us to follow in God's marvelous book. Read Luke 6:27–31. Ask yourself, "Am I following these directions? If I do, what will happen? Maybe another miracle?"

Hmm, I wonder!

LORD,

Help me follow your directions
and trust you for the outcome.

ACTIVITIES

Week 1

Mom

This month we will take some directions from the Bible and put them to work. When we outwardly follow the Lord's directions, surprising things happen inwardly.

"Bless those who curse you, pray for those who mistreat you" (Luke 6:28). Do you know someone who doesn't seem to like you or anything you do? Is there someone who always tries to annoy you? Write the person's name on a 3 x 5 card and put it where you will see it at least once a day. Whenever you see it, pray for the person. My pastor says the only way to bless someone is to pray for his or her well-being and happiness. That's right. No complaining to God and no asking Him to remake the person to your liking. You must pray for the person's good and well-being.

After a week of earnest prayer for your enemy, record your feelings about the person.

Mom & Me

Tools: construction paper, pen and pencil, crayons or markers.

1. Make two identical connect-the-dots puzzles. (See sample on page 153.) (It will be easier to draw the star, number the dots, then trace the numbers and dots onto another piece of paper.) This looks like an ordinary connect-the-dots puzzle, but it's not. If you try to do it without following the directions you will get a mess.

2. Give your child one puzzle without any directions and have her try to figure it out. When she gives up, give her a second copy along with the following directions.

3. Connect these pairs of dots with a straight line:

1–4	6–7	3–5	12–15
2–13	13–7	9–11	6–14
8–10	2–14		

4. **Ask:** *Did it turn out to be what you thought it would be? Does your picture remind you of someone in the Bible who followed God's directions? Remember the kings who followed the star to Bethlehem?* *(continued on page 157)*

MATTHEW 5:16

*In the same way, let your light
shine before men, that they may
see your good deeds and praise
your Father in heaven.*

PRAY *EVERY* DAY

1.
2.
3.
4.

SUNDAY

MONDAY

TUESDAY

WEDNESDAY

THURSDAY

FRIDAY

SATURDAY

ACTIVITIES

Week 2

Mom

"Give to everyone who asks you, and if anyone takes what belongs to you, do not demand it back" (Luke 6:30). The first thing that comes to my mind when I read this verse is a parking place! It is such an insignificant thing, and it doesn't belong to anyone, but it is often a sore spot. I have seen verbal abuse and physical violence erupt over a parking place. Maybe you lose patience when someone takes your place in line at a traffic light or a cash register. When someone takes what you think is yours this week remind yourself of this verse. It will ease some of life's tense moments and help you become a more gracious person.

Mom & Me

Tools: bowls, spoons, measuring utensils, small amounts of margarine, white and brown sugar, eggs, baking soda, salt, vanilla flavoring, chocolate chips.

1. Tell your child you would like a cookie. If she volunteers to make you one, point at the bowl and ingredients and **say:** *Okay, make me a cookie.* Some children will throw things into the bowl and have a wonderful time mixing ingredients. DON'T INTERFERE. Let her produce something that leaves her thinking she should have had help.

2. If your child is more timid (or if she realizes she needs directions) skip the experimental stage and discuss the importance of following the right directions.

3. **Explain:** *God made each of us and He knows better than anybody what directions will make our lives turn out right. For example, He knows that telling lies will cause trouble, so in the Bible, His book of directions, He says that we should always tell the truth. God knows the best directions for our lives! Let's talk about other things God tells us in His book while we make these cookies.*

4. **Directions:**

    Heat oven to 375. In small bowl combine 1 cup and 2 T. flour, 1/2 t. salt, 1/2 t. baking soda. In large bowl combine 1/2 cup but-

(continued on page 157)

MATTHEW 5:16

*In the same way, let your light
shine before men, that they may
see your good deeds and praise
your Father in heaven.*

PRAY *EVERY* DAY

1.
2.
3.
4.

SUNDAY

MONDAY

TUESDAY

WEDNESDAY

THURSDAY

FRIDAY

SATURDAY

 **ACTIVITIES**

Week 3

Mom

"Give, and it will be given to you. A good measure, pressed down, shaken together and running over, will be poured into your lap. For with the measure you use, it will be measured to you" (Luke 6:38). Be a secret giver this week. Deliver your best to someone who doesn't expect it. Be generous until it hurts! Tuck some money into an envelope, take it to church with you, and give it to somebody, quietly. Give this direction a chance. Pray about it.

Mom & Me

Tools: flashlight, Bible.

1. Take your child with you into a closet or bathroom that can be completely darkened.
2. Sit in the darkness for a few minutes and talk about what it would be like if the world was always so dark. Discuss why light is so important.
3. Turn on your flashlight and read Matthew 5:14–16. **Explain:** *This is a direction Jesus gave us to follow. We can be light by helping others see Jesus and by helping them find the way to Him.*
4. Read John 8:12.
5. Sing "This Little Light of Mine."
6. Review the memory verse, update your prayer list, and pray together. Ask God to help you let your light shine.

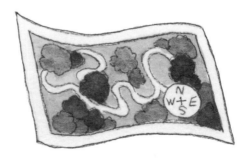

MATTHEW 5:16
In the same way, let your light
shine before men, that they may
see your good deeds and praise
your Father in heaven.

PRAY *EVERY* DAY
1.
2.
3.
4.

SUNDAY

MONDAY

TUESDAY

WEDNESDAY

THURSDAY

FRIDAY

SATURDAY

ACTIVITIES

Week 4

Mom

Repeat last week's exercise. This time give something to a stranger. Practice makes perfect! (Be sure to give God the glory.)

Mom & Me

1. Review some of your family's safety rules. **Explain:** *One of God's directions is for children to obey their parents (Eph. 6:1). God wants you to be safe, and Mom and Dad have some rules to keep you safe.*

2. Suggested reading:

    Obedience, What Is It? Jane Buerger, The Child's World

    Keep an Eye on Kevin (Safety Begins at Home), Genevieve Gray, Lothrop, Lee & Shepard

    Katie's Adventure at Blueberry Pond, Ann Neilsen, Chariot Books

    Why Do I Do Things Wrong? Carolyn Nystrom, Moody

    The Son Who Said He Wouldn't, Louise Ulmer, Concordia Press

3. Review the memory verse, update your prayer list, and pray together.

MATTHEW 5:16

*In the same way, let your light
shine before men, that they may
see your good deeds and praise
your Father in heaven.*

PRAY *EVERY* **DAY**

1.
2.
3.
4.

SUNDAY

MONDAY

TUESDAY

WEDNESDAY

THURSDAY

FRIDAY

SATURDAY

Trusting God's Promises

JULY

Never will I leave you; never will I forsake you.

HEBREWS 13:5

JUST FOR MOM

I GLANCED AT THE big story book my sons had chosen for me to read, and then at the clock. Two hours after bedtime. The story would have to wait until tomorrow.

"But you promised, Mom!"

"I know, but that was before I knew we'd be out so late!"

It's not that I try to break promises, or even that I make them carelessly. I mean well. I intend to keep my word, but I do not know what the future holds, not even the next moment. I really have no business making promises at all!

A promise is not simply something we hope will come to pass. Nor is it something we will do our best to make happen. A promise is something that *will* come to pass. And who but God has the power to guarantee the future? Oh, we can make some pretty good guesses. It seems safe to promise that the sun will rise in the morning. But the sun is not under our control, and we have no business promising what we have no power to bring about.

We throw around promises far too casually! In doing so we teach that a promise means "I'll do the best I can to see that it happens." If that is what we mean to say, that is what we should say! A promise is something that *will* come to pass ... no doubt about it!

If we water down the meaning of promise, we risk losing our sense of the power of the promises God has

given us. He promised a Savior would come to Israel, and it happened. He said the Savior would be from David's family, would teach and heal, and would suffer, die, and rise from the dead, as it happened. He promised the Holy Spirit would come to His disciples, as it happened on Pentecost, and He promised the same Spirit to us (Acts 2:38–39).

God's promises are not to be taken lightly. They are more reliable than anything else we trust. In fact, God never breaks His promises.

LORD,

Thank you that your promises are more sure than the rising of the sun and the changing of the seasons.

ACTIVITIES

Week 1

Mom

Read 2 Corinthians 6:18. The God who created life and all living things has promised to be our Father. He could have promised to be our keeper or our master. He could have promised to hold us in subjection like a slave. But He promised to be our Father. The role of Father in Scripture is to care for the needs of His children, to discipline them, and to love them.

How are we to respond to such a promise? Think of the implications of having God as your Father. Read 2 Corinthians 7:1. Record your thoughts in a notebook.

Mom & Me

Tools: construction paper; crayons, markers, paint, glitter, sequins, or brightly colored paper; glue.

1. **Explain:** *Long ago, God promised a man named Noah that He would never again destroy the earth with a worldwide flood, as He did in Noah's day. As a reminder of that promise God put a rainbow in the sky. Now every time we see a rainbow we remember God's promise that He has kept for thousands of years. Can you think of some of God's other promises?*

   One promise God made to us is that He will be our Father. He promised never to leave us and always to take care of us. And He promised that we will live forever with Him if we believe in Jesus. I believe in God's promises! Do you believe God's promises?

2. Draw a promise rainbow. (See the sample on page 154.) Help your child think of ways to make this promise rainbow especially beautiful. You could paint it, paste glitter or sequins on it, or cut up some brightly colored paper and glue little pieces in the rainbow stripes.

3. Any day this month that you or your child tells somebody about one of God's promises, mark the special day with a picture of a rainbow or a rainbow sticker.

4. Review the memory verse together, update your prayer list, and pray together. Remember to thank God for keeping His promises.

HEBREWS 13:5
Never will I leave you; never will I forsake you.

PRAY *EVERY* DAY
1.
2.
3.
4.

SUNDAY

MONDAY

TUESDAY

WEDNESDAY

THURSDAY

FRIDAY

SATURDAY

ACTIVITIES

Week 2

Mom

When Paul faced weaknesses that slowed him down, he asked God to heal him. God responded with another promise. Read 2 Corinthians 12:9.

We can claim this promise for our own even though God gave it to our brother Paul. God knows what is best for our lives, and He knows how our lives will best glorify Him. When things don't go the way we think they should, it's okay to ask God to remove our weakness and to bring healing, but remember the promise that followed Paul's request. Trust in that promise and trust God to know what is best.

Mom & Me

Tools: blindfold

1. Ask your child if he trusts you. Discuss what trust means.
2. Ask him to go on a trust walk with you. Blindfold him and tell him he can relax and trust you because you will not let go of his hand or let him fall or trip.
3. Walk around your house. Watch out for any obstacles and warn him of holes, stairs, or things to step around.
4. Remove the blindfold. Talk about the experience and discuss what you've learned about trust.
5. **Explain:** *There is probably nobody in the world you can trust as much as you trust Mom and Dad. We love you and will protect you. You have learned to trust us because when we say we will take care of you, we do. But there is someone you can trust even more than you trust Dad and me, and that is Jesus. God has always kept His promises, ever since the beginning of the world. He has never forgotten to do anything He said He would do. Sometimes Dad and I forget things. Things don't always work out the way we want them to. We always do the best we can, but sometimes we can't make everything work out right. But God always makes things turn out just the way He said they would.*
6. Review the memory verse, update your prayer list, and pray together.

HEBREWS 13:5
Never will I leave you; never will I forsake you.

PRAY *EVERY* DAY
1.
2.
3.
4.

SUNDAY

MONDAY

TUESDAY

WEDNESDAY

THURSDAY

FRIDAY

SATURDAY

ACTIVITIES

Week 3

Mom

Read Hebrews 13:5–6. Can you imagine anything better than the promise that God will not leave you? No power anywhere can undo this promise. Keep it in mind everywhere you go this week. You are not alone!

Mom & Me

Tools: Paper, pencil.

1. Divide the paper into seven boxes and label the boxes with the days of the week.

2. **Ask:** *What would you think if I promised you a special treat and then changed my mind and said you couldn't have it? What if I told you to wait for me at a special place and then I didn't come for you? What if I promised to take care of you but didn't fix you anything to eat when you were hungry and didn't wash your clothes when they got dirty? How would you feel?*

3. **Explain:** *If these things happened you would never believe anything I said. And if you couldn't believe me you wouldn't trust me. And if you couldn't trust me you would be afraid to obey me. And if you were in danger and didn't obey me, you might get hurt. That is why it is important for me to be trustworthy. It is also important for you to learn to be trustworthy. That is why we are practicing trustworthiness this month.*

4. Have your child choose a task that he will perform every day this week. (It could be the same task every day or a different one.) Write the task(s) in the appropriate boxes on the contract you have prepared.

5. On the bottom of the contract write, "With God's help I will try to do these things." Have your child sign his name at the bottom.

6. Put the contract in a visible place. Pray about it together.

7. Be generous with your praise this week. Help your child feel the pride and joy that come from doing a job well.

8. Review the memory verse, update your prayer list, and pray together.

HEBREWS 13:5
Never will I leave you; never will I forsake you.

PRAY *EVERY* DAY
1.
2.
3.
4.

SUNDAY

MONDAY

TUESDAY

WEDNESDAY

THURSDAY

FRIDAY

SATURDAY

ACTIVITIES

Week 4

Mom

Read Romans 8:28–39. When you come to the end, stand up and shout, "Amen!" (You can substitute "All right!" "Yeah!" or any other affirmation that suits you.) What a promise! Nothing will ever separate us from God's love! God promised it, and He doesn't break His promises!

Share that promise with somebody today.

Mom & Me

1. **Ask:** *Do you trust the chair you are sitting on?* **Explain:** *This chair has held you every time you have sat on it, so now you don't even think about whether or not it will hold you. God is like that. He never lets us down. We can always trust Him to take care of us.*

2. Suggested reading:
   Noah's Ark, Catherine Chase, Dandelion Press
   God, You Are Always With Us, Carrie Lou Goddard, Abingdon Press
   Angels and Me, Carolyn Nystrom, Moody
   Do Angels Go Camping? Donna Perugini, Harrison House

3. Review the memory verse, update your prayer list, and pray together.

HEBREWS 13:5

Never will I leave you; never will I forsake you.

PRAY *EVERY* DAY
1.
2.
3.
4.

SUNDAY

MONDAY

TUESDAY

WEDNESDAY

THURSDAY

FRIDAY

SATURDAY

Watching
Our
Words

AUGUST

May the words of my mouth and the meditation of my heart be pleasing in your sight, O LORD, my Rock and my Redeemer.

PSALM 19:14

Pet Show
Today
No Frogs
Please!

🍎 JUST FOR MOM 🍎

O NE SUNNY MORNING I had
my large, upright vacuum balanced about half way up
our front stairs so I could reach the top stair with the at-
tachment hose. The noise of the vacuum and the hum of
the dishwasher made it difficult for me to hear two-year-
old Michael at the foot of the stairs.

"What?" I yelled.

He said it again, but still not loud enough for me to
hear. "What?" I hollered again.

Michael mounted the first stair and tried again, but to
no avail. He began climbing toward me, and I saw that
he was headed for trouble. The vacuum-cleaner cord
was tangled around his feet, and each move he made
caused the vacuum to waver on its stair. With visions of
the machine falling on top of him and the two of them
crashing down the stairs I yelled to him to stop!

"What?" he said, also unable to hear.

"Get down these stairs right now!" I screeched.

Finally hearing what I said, he turned his angelic little
face toward mine and, with a determined half-grin,
responded, "No!"

Something snapped. I was no longer the hard-work-
ing Mommy who balances large machines in precarious
places and worries about the safety of her child. I was a
Mommy whose authority had been challenged! As I
reached for the vacuum I upset the balance, and the
machine began to fall directly toward Michael! I grabbed
the handle and averted the crash, but a muscle in my

neck disapproved of my quick movement and filled me with immediate and intense pain.

"Michael Andrew, you go to your room NOW! And don't you ever say no to Mommy again!" I bellowed.

Mikey broke into tears, stamped his foot, and said, "No!"

Who knows what drives a supposedly mature adult and a usually sweet child to stand toe to toe and yell into each other's faces about something neither understands?

In a matter of minutes reason returned, we settled the conflict, and sat hugging each other on the bottom stair. We forgave each other and Mike ran off to play.

I walked into the dining room and glanced out the open window. In the driveway stood two of my neighbors. More damage had been done than I first realized. Mikey and I emerged from the battle relatively unscathed, but my Christian testimony had indeed gone right out the window!

I walked out to say a casual hi to them and to explain the unfriendly noises they had undoubtedly heard. I thought of the times I had tried to witness to them. The best I could do now was confess that I had lost my control and assure them that Mikey and I were friends once more. How I wished I could grab back those words I had let loose at Michael! I returned to my vacuuming with one prayer on my lips ...

LORD,

I'm sorry! Please help me control my tongue!

ACTIVITIES

Week 1

Mom

Even though my words themselves may not be bad, my sarcasm and nasty voice inflections can be just as bad as bad words. On the days I wake up with self-control on my mind and I fix my sights on a day without even one little slip, I usually realize over my morning coffee that I've blown it already!

This is such a difficult subject that a full week of preparation in prayer is warranted. Read Psalm 19. Write verse 14 on a 3 x 5 card and tape it to your bathroom mirror: "May the words of my mouth and the meditation of my heart be acceptable in your sight, O LORD, my Rock and my Redeemer." Repeat it each morning this week and keep it in your mind throughout the day.

Mom & Me

Tools: construction paper, crayons or markers.

1. Fill the page with drawings of happy faces with word balloons next to them. (See sample on page 154.)
2. **Explain:** *Some words are good and bring happiness. Some words cause sadness.* **Ask:** *What kind of things do you like people to say to you? What kind of words does God want to hear us say?*
3. Write good and kind phrases in the empty balloons. (Suggestions: I love you. You are my friend. God loves you. Can I help? I made this for you. Will you be my friend? Do you want to play?)
4. Color the pictures.
5. Each time one of you catches a bad word before it comes out and replaces it with a good word, tell about the experience and mark the day with a sticker or a picture of a smiley face.
6. Review the memory verse, update your prayer list, and pray together. Emphasize saying nice things.

PSALM 19:14
May the words of my mouth and the meditation of my heart be pleasing in your sight, O LORD, my Rock and my Redeemer.

PRAY *EVERY* **DAY**
1.
2.
3.
4.

SUNDAY

MONDAY

TUESDAY

WEDNESDAY

THURSDAY

FRIDAY

SATURDAY

ACTIVITIES

Week 2

Mom

Read Psalm 139. David is realizing just how well God knows him. His words apply to us too! There is not one little thing about us that God doesn't already know. He knows our daily problems and challenges, and He can and will help us with each one. Pay particular attention to verse 4.

Keep last week's card up for a reminder. Make a conscious effort this week to stop any unkind words before they move from your thoughts to your mouth. Pay close attention to the words you use to discipline your kids. Remember that your tone of voice says a lot!

Mom & Me

Tools: dark construction paper, pen or pencil, tube of toothpaste.

1. Write the word *WORD* in big letters on the construction paper. Talk about what a word is and why words are important to us.
2. Ask your child to trace with toothpaste the word you have written on the construction paper. Talk about how easy it is to get the word to come out of the tube.
3. Now ask her to take the word back. Explain that you want her to erase the word by putting it back in the tube. When she gives up, **explain:** *It is very easy to let our words come out, but once we say them we can never take them back! We must be very careful to watch the words we say, and to never say words that will hurt other people or God.*
4. Talk about words that are good and words that hurt.
5. Review the memory verse, update your prayer list, and pray together. Ask God to help you choose words that are good.

PSALM 19:14
May the words of my mouth and
the meditation of my heart be
pleasing in your sight, O LORD, my
Rock and my Redeemer.

PRAY *EVERY* **DAY**
1.
2.
3.
4.

SUNDAY

MONDAY

TUESDAY

WEDNESDAY

THURSDAY

FRIDAY

SATURDAY

 ACTIVITIES

Week 3

Mom

Read Matthew 12:36–37. Ouch! What good is it to be known as a Christian if we are also known for our gossip and unkind words. As Christians we ought not simply act nice; our words must reflect the change brought about by the Holy Spirit!

At work or with friends this week, be on the lookout for the testimony of your words. We may not always notice our own slander, gossip, crude humor, or unkind remarks, but we can be sure the Devil will see that others notice them!

Mom & Me

Tools: small box of candy, cookies, or raisins; small stones, dirt, and sticks.

Advance preparation: Buy a small box of a treat your child enjoys. Carefully open the box, remove the treat, and replace it with stones or sticks (something of the same weight and consistency so the box will feel as if the treat is still in it and sound the same if it is shaken).

1. Put the box where your child can see it. Tell her she can have it if she can tell you what is in it. Elicit as many descriptive words about the treat as you can.
2. Give your child the box and tell her to open it.
3. Have her describe what is inside. (Produce the real treat from your pocket if you detect tears.)
4. **Explain:** *It doesn't make any difference what the box looks like if what is inside is yucky. It's the same with people. It doesn't matter if we are pretty or wear nice clothes if what is inside us is not nice. This week let's try to make nice words come out of our mouths. If we need to remind each other, let's say, "Remember the treat!"*
5. Review the memory verse, update your prayer list, and pray together.

PSALM 19:14
May the words of my mouth and
the meditation of my heart be
pleasing in your sight, O LORD, my
Rock and my Redeemer.

PRAY *EVERY* DAY
1.
2.
3.
4.

SUNDAY

MONDAY

TUESDAY

WEDNESDAY

THURSDAY

FRIDAY

SATURDAY

ACTIVITIES

Week 4

Mom

Read Colossians 3:17. Make it your challenge this week and for the rest of your life!

Mom & Me

1. Before storytime, take turns saying one nice thing about each person in your family. Saying good things about people is fun!
2. Suggested reading:
   Let's Talk About Being Bossy, Joy Wilt Berry, Children's Press
   What Do You Say, Dear? Sesyle Joslin, Young Scott Books
   The Thingamajig Book of Manners, Irene Keller, Children's Press
3. Review the memory verse, update your prayer list, and pray together.

PSALM 19:14

May the words of my mouth and
the meditation of my heart be
pleasing in your sight, O LORD, my
Rock and my Redeemer.

PRAY *EVERY* **DAY**
1.
2.
3.
4.

SUNDAY

MONDAY

TUESDAY

WEDNESDAY

THURSDAY

FRIDAY

SATURDAY

Seeing God's Miracles

SEPTEMBER

*In the beginning God created
the heavens and the earth.*
GENESIS 1:1

JUST FOR MOM

WE WALKED HOME from the school carnival with two plastic bags, each holding about two cups of water and a tiny fish.

"Don't be upset if they only last a few days," I warned, trying gently to let my excited children in on the realities of survival for goldfish.

To my surprise, the fish lasted several weeks in their peanut butter jar ... right up to summer vacation. When time came to drive to Michigan, Jon put the lid on the jar and put the fish in the car for the fourteen-hour ride. They seemed none the worse for wear when we arrived at Grandma's. I found myself hoping they would be around awhile longer. You can talk to fish, you know. It is more acceptable than talking to yourself, and fish never disagree with you.

After vacation we again sealed the jar and stuck it in the trunk for the journey home. They both probably would have survived the trip had we remembered to take them out of the trunk when we got home.

Because she had survived such an awful ordeal, because of her deepening gold color, and because we saw Golda Meir on the evening news, Jon decided to give our surviving fish a name. She became Golda My Fish.

We found a large glass globe for her and we accepted her as part of our family. I kept her bowl on the ledge above the kitchen sink and often found comfort in her company as I cleaned up the dishes.

We were well into our second year with Golda when

Kevin came into my room one morning to tell me that she was swimming on her side. Sure enough, our lovely fish was floating near the top of her bowl, moving only occasionally in a circle. Kevin stood near her bowl and offered encouragement in his sweet voice, "Come on, Golda, you can do it! Just wiggle a little!"

I watched as the hope drained from his eyes. Finally Golda was still. With a bit more ceremony than her bowl-mate had received, we buried Golda at sea.

Such a simple thing ... a goldfish. Yet she had something that all our fancy toys and gadgets lack. Life. She was unique. She was an original, living creation!

"But God chose the foolish things of the world to shame the wise; God chose the weak things of the world to shame the strong ... so that no one may boast before him" (1 Corinthians 1:27–29).

On the evening news I hear people brag about their accomplishments. I hear the super-powers compare strength and dare each other to prove their superiority. I hear about scientific breakthroughs and humanitarian gestures, but I hear nothing about my goldfish.

Silly, you say. But is it? Can science create a single goldfish? Can the super-powers, with all their power to kill, cause this little creature to live again?

LORD,

Your wonder is all around us, but we are so blind! Our grandest accomplishments pale in comparison to your simplest creations.

107

ACTIVITIES

Week 1

Mom

Read Genesis 1:1–8 and 14–19. How long has it been since you sat outside and watched the stars? We don't ordinarily give much thought to the sun or the moon. Every evening this week, locate the moon and notice how it changes from Monday to Saturday. Do some star gazing and notice how many suns and stars speckle the sky. Watch for falling stars and locate the Milky Way. God created all this by speaking a command. Praise Him!

Mom & Me

Tools: small piece of paper, markers, ink pad or acrylic paint.

1. **Explain:** *You are one of God's best creations. God made you different from everybody else in the whole world. Some of us look like other people in the family, but there is only one of each of us. God made us just the way we are.*

2. Press your child's thumb into the ink pad or paint and help him make a thumbprint in the middle of the paper. Let it dry. Now use the markers to make it into some kind of creature (e.g., person, bug, animal, etc. See the sample on page 154).

3. **Explain:** *This month we'll be looking for some of God's creations that are new to you. There are lots of bugs, flowers, plants, and animals that you have never seen before. Maybe we'll buy a new kind of fruit that you have never tasted.*

4. When you find one of God's creations that is new to you, thank Him for it and mark the special find on your calendar with a sticker, a picture, or a thumbprint.

5. Review the memory verse together, update your prayer list, and pray together. Thank God for His wonderful creation.

GENESIS 1:1

In the beginning God created the heavens and the earth.

PRAY *EVERY* DAY
1.
2.
3.
4.

SUNDAY

MONDAY

TUESDAY

WEDNESDAY

THURSDAY

FRIDAY

SATURDAY

ACTIVITIES

Week 2

Mom

Read Genesis 1:10–13. Observe a tree this week. Try to figure out how water and dirt turn into wood as the tree takes nourishment from the ground. How do buds know when to form and flowers know when to turn into fruit? Consider the way the leaves grow and turn green, then orange or red, and then fall to the ground to become food for the tree. Look for 100 kinds of plants in your neighborhood. Try to figure out why spinach tastes different than a carrot! God created all this by speaking a command! Praise Him!

Mom & Me

Tools: Bible.

1. Discuss what it means to create something.
2. **Explain:** *Beautiful paintings, gardens, buildings, music, and stories are all created by people like you and me. But no one can create anything without using God's creation to do it. We can't color unless we have paper and crayons. We can't make music without an instrument or a voice. We can't even think up a new story without the thoughts and words God gives us, or without the brains in our heads. We can't even create a hug and a kiss without using something God made—our arms and lips.*

    God is the only one who can create anything new. The world, stars, planets, sun, moon, water, land, birds, fish, animals, bugs, and people all came right out of God's mind. He thought it all up and then spoke the words "Let there be ... " and all of the world happened just as He wanted it.

    Let's find out how God created the world.
3. Read Genesis 1. Look around the room to see how many things God created. Thank God for all He has made!
4. Review the memory verse, update your prayer list, and pray together.

GENESIS 1:1

In the beginning God created the
heavens and the earth.

PRAY *EVERY* DAY

1.
2.
3.
4.

SUNDAY

MONDAY

TUESDAY

WEDNESDAY

THURSDAY

FRIDAY

SATURDAY

ACTIVITIES

Week 3

Mom

Read Genesis 1:20–23. Watch a bird and try to understand how it flies. How do all the birds of the same species know the right song to sing? Watch a fish and try to understand how it breathes water! Go to the fish market and look closely at a lobster or a squid. God created all of them by speaking a command! Praise Him!

Mom & Me

Tools: paper, pencil.

1. Plan a visit to a grocery store with a lobster tank and plenty of fresh fruits and vegetables.
2. On the way there explain that you are on a special mission to find some of God's most unusual creations.
3. Make a list of all the unusual items you find. Smell and touch as many as you can.
4. Allow your child to buy a kind of fruit he has never tasted before.
5. On the way home discuss all the neat things you discovered.
6. Review the memory verse, update your prayer list, and pray together. Thank God for making so much variety.

GENESIS 1:1

In the beginning God created the heavens and the earth.

PRAY *EVERY* **DAY**

1.
2.
3.
4.

SUNDAY

MONDAY

TUESDAY

WEDNESDAY

THURSDAY

FRIDAY

SATURDAY

ACTIVITIES

Week 4

Mom

Read Genesis 1:24–31. Pet a dog or a cat. What makes a dog a dog and a cat a cat? Why do they like us to pet them? Think about the stranger animals, like the hippo, the sea lion, or the armadillo. What kind of a sense of humor does God have? Look at a spider or an ant. Look at your own body and realize its complexity. God created all of us by speaking a command. Praise Him!

Mom & Me

1. Before storytime, ask your child to tell you as much as he can about the best things God has created. As you listen, think about how his mind is developing!

2. Suggested reading:

   God's World Makes Me Feel So Little, Helen Caswell, Abingdon Press

   Six Busy Days (The Wonderful Creation Story), Mary E. Erickson, Chariot Books

   What Does God Do? (text from International Children's Bible), Hans Wilhelm, Worthy Press

3. Review the memory verse, update your prayer list, and pray together.

GENESIS 1:1

In the beginning God created the heavens and the earth.

PRAY *EVERY* DAY
1.
2.
3.
4.

SUNDAY

MONDAY

TUESDAY

WEDNESDAY

THURSDAY

FRIDAY

SATURDAY

Lending
A
Hand

OCTOBER

*In everything, do to others
what you would have them do
to you, for this sums up the
Law and the Prophets.*

MATTHEW 7:12

JUST FOR MOM

THE PAIN IN MY HEAD would have been more bearable if I hadn't been so scared about its cause. My doctor said it might be a reaction to some medication, but we could do nothing but wait and see.

Wait and see? Me? Who would feed my children and drive them to all of their activities? The laundry needed washing, the house needed cleaning, shopping had to be done, and I had obligations at church that wouldn't wait! My schedule didn't even allow for a coffee break, and there I sat ... alone ... with no telephone and no calendar ... just me!

I cried tears I had been saving for years. They kept falling as I faced the awful realization that my husband, kids, house, and church would all survive the night without me.

When a friend appeared at the door I tried to send him away. He came in. I told him I was fine. He kept asking how I was. I told him jokes. He didn't laugh. I said I wanted to be alone. He held my hand until I couldn't stand being strong any longer. He let me cry, and when I looked into his eyes I saw tears.

Whatever my doctor and the hospital staff did to make me well was insignificant compared to the healing my friend, Ralph, brought me. He obeyed Romans 12:15, "weep with those who weep," and I thank God for him!

Kind words and cheerful admonitions to "look on the bright side" do not always help a hurt. Sometimes only tears can help, and sometimes we cannot shed those

tears alone. The tears that fell when I was alone were bitter. Those that flowed as a result of my friend's loving touch were cleansing.

Sometimes we need to cry. Strength and a great attitude are not things we achieve on our own. Matthew 11:28 urges us to "Come to me, all you who are weary and burdened, and I will give you rest." Sometimes the only way to give our burdens to the Lord is with the help of a loving friend. There is no shame in weakness unless we hide it and insist we are strong.

LORD,

Use my hands to help those trying to carry burdens too heavy for them to bear.

ACTIVITIES

Week 1

Mom

Be on the alert this week for ways the Lord can use your hands. Watch for someone who is ill and needs help cleaning the house or doing laundry. Look for an elderly person who needs to have leaves raked or windows washed. Watch for a new mother who would give her right arm for an hour or two all by herself. Lend a hand. This may be the most fun you've had this year.

Mom & Me

Tools: construction paper, pencil or pen.

1. Have your child place both hands on a blank sheet of construction paper. Trace around them. Have her add fingernails, wrinkles, rings, and maybe a watch to make her hands look really neat. (See sample on page 155.)
2. Discuss ways that God can use our hands. **Ask:** *Can you wave to your neighbors and say hi? Can you help carry the groceries? Can you make your bed and put away your clothes? Can you make a special card for your favorite uncle or aunt?*
3. Whenever you use your hands for God this month, mark the day with a sticker or a picture of a hand.
4. Review the memory verse, update your prayer list, and pray together. Ask God to show you ways you can lend a hand.

MATTHEW 7:12

In everything, do to others what
you would have them do to you,
for this sums up the Law and the
Prophets.

PRAY *EVERY* **DAY**
1.
2.
3.
4.

SUNDAY

MONDAY

TUESDAY

WEDNESDAY

THURSDAY

FRIDAY

SATURDAY

ACTIVITIES

Week 2

Mom

Call someone this week who has undergone some kind of personal crisis and tell him or her you'd like to listen. It is very hard to keep from giving advice or passing on what you hear, but you must avoid both! A good listener does just that ... listens. You may have a new friend by the end of this week.

Mom & Me

Tools: Bible.

1. Read the Golden Rule in Matthew 7:12.
2. Use the following role-playing situations or adapt them so your child will understand. If she does or says something unsuitable, say, "Now let's change parts," and show her a more Christian solution to the problem.
3. **Explain:** *Today we are going to be actors and actresses. I will explain a situation and then we will pretend it is happening to us. Remember, Jesus says we should treat others the same way we want them to treat us. We'll try to act the way Jesus would want us to.*

   a. You and I are shopping and you see a toy that you really want to have! You ask me but I say you may not have the toy today.

   b. Your little brother gets into your best toys! When he hears you coming he gets nervous and tries to put them away fast. One of your toys breaks. Your brother feels really bad about it and says he is sorry.

   c. Grandma always sends you a card for Valentine's Day. This morning your sister got a card from Grandma but you did not.

   d. You are with a group of kids at church while the adults are in a meeting upstairs. Suddenly a thunderstorm comes up and you see that one of the kids is about to cry.

   e. Just outside of the market you see an old lady drop her purse. One of her dollar bills has fallen under her cart and she doesn't see it there. You can see it. *(continued on page 158)*

MATTHEW 7:12

In everything, do to others what you would have them do to you, for this sums up the Law and the Prophets.

PRAY *EVERY* DAY

1.
2.
3.
4.

SUNDAY

MONDAY

TUESDAY

WEDNESDAY

THURSDAY

FRIDAY

SATURDAY

ACTIVITIES

Mom

This week we will be lending the other ear! This week seek out someone who has just experienced a personal triumph and be a listener for them. Sometimes the joy that could be experienced through a personal accomplishment is greatly diminished by the fact that nobody really wants to hear about it! Such jealousy has no place between Christian brothers and sisters! (Remember, Romans 12:15 says to rejoice with those who rejoice as well as weep with those who mourn!)

Mom & Me

1. Discuss the importance of being a good listener.
2. Ask your child to tell you about an experience that made her feel very happy. Listen attentively as she recalls the event. Ask questions. Show particular interest in the details. Thank her for sharing the story when she finishes.
3. Plan a visit with an elderly person. Pray about your visit before you go.
4. Ask your child to try to get the person to tell about an experience that made him or her very happy. Practice your listening skills. (If your child is shy, work as a team in asking the questions.) What could be more welcome than a story of happiness shared in this way? God may bless you all unexpectedly in this activity.
5. Review the memory verse, update your prayer list, and pray together.

MATTHEW 7:12

In everything, do to others what
you would have them do to you,
for this sums up the Law and the
Prophets.

PRAY *EVERY* DAY

1.
2.
3.
4.

SUNDAY

MONDAY

TUESDAY

WEDNESDAY

THURSDAY

FRIDAY

SATURDAY

ACTIVITIES

Week 4

Mom

This week, look into your own home. Help your child with a chore she doesn't like to do, or make your child a special treat because that's how Jesus wants us to treat each other. Maybe you could ask her what you could do for her as a special favor ... maybe take her to lunch or make new covers for her school books. Be creative. Have fun. What better way to model the Golden Rule than by using it on our own kids!

Mom & Me

1. Read Luke 10:29–37 with your child. **Explain:** *This is a story that Jesus told to teach the people the way God wanted them to act.*
2. Suggested reading:
     Peter's Chair, Ezra Jack Keats, Harper & Row
     A Super Friend, Dandi D. Knorr, Standard Publishing Company
     Who Is My Neighbor? Joan Lowery Nixon, Concordia
3. Review the memory verse, update your prayer list, and pray together.

MATTHEW 7:12

In everything, do to others what
you would have them do to you,
for this sums up the Law and the
Prophets.

PRAY *EVERY* DAY

1.
2.
3.
4.

SUNDAY

MONDAY

TUESDAY

WEDNESDAY

THURSDAY

FRIDAY

SATURDAY

Spreading God's Love

NOVEMBER

We love because he first loved us.
                    1 JOHN 4:19

JUST FOR MOM

ON A GRAY DAY between the last
of the orange leaves and the first of the white snow, the
older kids left for school in a gray kind of mood. Mikey
stayed home in much the same state of mind. Something
had to be done! I sneaked around the kitchen, feeling
my mood lighten at the prospect of surprising everybody
with the treat I had in mind!

As I formed the dough in the bowl, the feel of it told
me it would be good! I slipped the towel-covered dough
into the warm oven to rise.

After an hour or so the dough had risen to a soft
mound. I punched it down so it could rise again. I
smiled as I put Mike down for his nap and tidied up the
house. The next hour zipped by. I formed the dough
into two loaves, covered them, and waited for them to
rise one last time. I hummed while I paid the bills. The
anticipation of this treat had really brightened my day! At
last the loaves were ready to bake!

The house filled with a wonderful aroma! The deli-
cious smell drew Kevin from the cartoon he started
watching after pre-school and Mikey from his nap. Then
the front door flew open and in raced Krista. "Bread! I
could smell it when I got off the bus!" she exclaimed.

I removed two beautiful brown loaves from the
oven, and we waited for them to cool slightly—the
longest ten minutes of the day. I sat the kids at the table
and sliced four, steamy pieces. We watched the butter
melt into the holes. Krista took the first bite.

"Something's wrong with this bread," she sputtered.

I took a bite of mine. The flat, bland taste surprised me. I took a second bite, but there was no improvement. What in the world was wrong? What could have happened to this great-looking, great-smelling bread?

Salt! I forgot salt! Just one teaspoon for two loaves, but what a difference it makes.

"Hey, we can fix this!" I assured the kids, and proceeded to haul out jelly, cinnamon sugar, and honey. But none of them could cover up my mistake. Nothing could take the place of the missing ingredient. Yuck! What good are two loaves of great-looking, great-smelling, horrible-tasting bread?

I fed the uneaten treat to the dog, and the kids left the table quietly, their excitement and enthusiasm dampened by disappointment.

Worldly enticement is a lot like my beautiful, tasteless bread. It promises satisfaction, but lacks the necessary ingredients. And no matter how we doctor it up, we cannot cover up the mistake of omitting the key flavoring ingredient. Like my bread, worldly success is unsatisfying without the salt.

Jesus said, "You are the salt of the earth" (Matthew 5:13). Jesus in us makes us salty, and without our saltiness, the world around us is bland and tasteless.

LORD,

Thank you for using me to flavor your world and make it a better place! Teach me to use your seasoning tastefully.

ACTIVITIES

Week 1

Mom

What makes a person who follows Christ different from any other nice person? The Beatitudes, found in Matthew 5:1–12, tell us. Some people call the Beatitudes the eight attitudes we are to cultivate, or the eight be-attitudes. These qualities make a person blessed ... or happy.

But even nice people cannot behave this way consistently without the power of the Spirit to make it possible. These characteristics make Christians unique. When we become like verses 1–12, we also become like verse 13! Familiarize yourself with these verses by reading them every day this week. Read them in several different translations if you can.

Mom & Me

Tools: black and blue construction paper, green pencil or marker, white glue, paper cup, Q-tip, salt

Advance preparation: Cut the blue paper into a six-inch circle (see the sample on page 155). Outline the land on your world with the green pencil or marker (no crayons).

1. Have your child color the world you have outlined. **Explain:** *This month we will be learning how God spreads His love in the world.*
2. Glue the world onto the black paper. **Explain:** *When God sent Jesus to the world, something special happened so that every person who believes in Jesus as God's Son becomes God's child. Jesus said it is our job, as His children, to spread His love. Jesus called people who spread God's love the salt of the earth.*
3. Give your child a paper cup. Mix equal parts of glue and water and let your child paint the land portion of the world with a Q-tip.
4. With undiluted glue, write "God's Love" above the world.
5. Let your child sprinkle salt so it covers all the wet, glued areas. Shake excess into the sink. Let your pretty "salted" world dry before you hang it up.
6. Review the memory verse. Update your prayer list and pray together.

1 JOHN 4:19
We love because he first loved us.

PRAY *EVERY* DAY
1.
2.
3.
4.

SUNDAY

MONDAY

TUESDAY

WEDNESDAY

THURSDAY

FRIDAY

SATURDAY

ACTIVITIES

Week 2

Mom

The word *blessed* appears nine times in Matthew 5:1–12, even though there are only eight beatitudes. The first eight refer to the way we are to respond to things that happen in our lives. They say, "Blessed are *the....*" *But verse 11 says, "Blessed are you when* they revile and persecute you...." This refers to something that *will*, not might, happen to us when we identify ourselves with Christ. Not a comforting thought is it? If we never experience verse 11, our identity as Christians may be too much of a secret.

This week look for ways to identify yourself as a Christian to the world. For example, I wear a small pin that is the sign of the fish (Icthus). When people ask me about it I have an opportunity to witness to them about what I believe.

Mom & Me

Tools: an eight-ounce glass of cold water for each person, fresh lemons (or a bottle of lemon juice), a lemon squeezer, sugar, measuring spoons, stirring spoons.

1. Distribute the water glasses and squeeze the lemons. Measure 1 1/2 teaspoons of lemon juice into each glass of water. Stir. Have everyone take a *tiny taste.*
2. Discuss what is wrong.
3. Add 2 teaspoons of sugar to each glass, stir until dissolved, and taste again.
4. **Explain:** *Even though we can't see it, sugar is important to lemonade.* **Ask:** *Can you think of some other ingredients we add to our food to make it taste good?*

    Jesus told His disciples they were the salt of the earth (Matt. 5:13). People who spread God's love are the salt of the earth because they make the world a better place to live. We may not look different, but the way we act will show others that Jesus has made us loving, like Him. We must be very careful how we act. Spreading God's love is an important job.

(continued on page 158)

1 JOHN 4:19
We love because he first loved us.

PRAY *EVERY* **DAY**
1.
2.
3.
4.

SUNDAY

MONDAY

TUESDAY

WEDNESDAY

THURSDAY

FRIDAY

SATURDAY

ACTIVITIES

Week 3

Mom

Read Colossians 4:5–6. We are the salt of the earth, but we won't be much good if we keep our saltiness to ourselves or sprinkle it out only when we are with other Christians. Also, salt is to be sprinkled sparingly, not dumped out all at once. Pray for opportunities to spread God's love and be salt for Him this week! Pray that He will show you when, where, and how to be a tasteful seasoning to the world around you. Spend this week preparing, and next week will be a real blessing.

Mom & Me

Tools: small glass jar, enough salt to fill the jar, food coloring, several small zip-loc plastic bags, toothpick.

1. Pour 1/4 cup salt into a bag. Add 2 or 3 drops of food coloring. Zip the bag closed and shake it up. Make several more colors of salt. Keep plenty of white salt.

2. Pour a layer of plain salt (about 1/4 inch) into the bottom of the jar. Pour a contrasting color on top of the first layer. Make layers of different colors until you are nearly to the top of the jar.

3. With the toothpick, poke through the layers next to the edge of the jar. This will make a pattern in the colored layers. Pull the toothpick out gently and repeat the process around the jar until you have made it pretty.

4. Fill the rest of the jar with uncolored salt and put the cap on tightly.

5. **Explain:** *We have made our jar of salt beautiful, and we are going to set it where everyone can see it so it can remind us that we are to be like salt—we are to make the world beautiful.*

6. **Ask:** *What did Jesus say was the salt of the earth?*

7. Review the memory verse, update your prayer list, and pray together.

1 JOHN 4:19
We love because he first loved us.

PRAY *EVERY* **DAY**
1.
2.
3.
4.

SUNDAY

MONDAY

TUESDAY

WEDNESDAY

THURSDAY

FRIDAY

SATURDAY

ACTIVITIES

Week 4

Mom

This week you are ready to act on last week's prayers. Perhaps you will have an opportunity to tell someone what the Lord has done in your life. Through volunteer work you may be able to explain your motives for trying to make your community a better place to live. By refusing to participate in an office gossip session, you might discourage others from doing it. By quietly saying grace at a social dinner, you might remind others that God is the ultimate provider.

Tell your children about any opportunity you have to spread God's love to the world. It is important that they see you actively spreading God's love and being the salt of the earth.

Mom & Me

1. Review what Jesus meant when He said, "You are the salt of the earth." Make sure your child knows how very special it is to spread God's love to others.
2. Suggested reading:
    Let's Talk About Being Rude, Joy Wilt Berry, Children's Press
    Fiddler, Stephen Cosgrove, Multnomah Press
    Jesus Is No Secret, Carolyn Nystrom, Moody
3. Review the memory verse, update your prayer list, and pray together.

1 JOHN 4:19
We love because he first loved us.

PRAY *EVERY* DAY
1.
2.
3.
4.

SUNDAY

MONDAY

TUESDAY

WEDNESDAY

THURSDAY

FRIDAY

SATURDAY

Giving Thanks To God

DECEMBER

For God so loved the world that he gave his one and only Son, that whoever believes in him shall not perish but have eternal life.

JOHN 3:16

🎁 JUST FOR MOM 🎁

AS I STOOD in the darkness an overwhelming feeling of love came over me. Tears coursed down my cheeks. Three beds held three warm, resting little bodies that had brought so much love into my life that such moments were almost too much to bear! I stroked a small blonde head, planted a kiss on a warm, pink cheek, brushed away my tears, and tried to pray. "Thank You, thank You ... " No other words would come. My heart ached with love for the children God had given me.

What mother hasn't had a similar experience? Who has never been overtaken by a sense of awe at the wonder of God's creation in the children placed into our care?

As the Christmas season approaches I think of the words of the familiar Christmas carol, "O come let us adore Him, Christ the Lord." Adoration is the feeling I have for my children. It goes beyond love or appreciation. It leaves me without words; none are adequate. This is how I am to feel about my Savior, Jesus!

As I prepare to celebrate Christ's birth this Christmas, I think of Jesus as a trusting, innocent child placed into a mother's care. I see Him as a delightful, inquisitive boy of twelve learning to be what His Father wanted Him to be. I see Him as a healthy, virile young man who carried love for the whole world inside His heart. I see Him as a trembling, tormented, innocent man who faced an awful death and yet took the time to pray for *me* (John 17:20–

23). I see Him dying and know that if our eyes had met at that moment, He would have known and loved *me*.

I think of all the stages of His life and remember that His Father watched it, allowed it, and suffered with Him through it all just for *me*. And then I see the empty tomb and hear His voice call my name in the garden.

Then, and only then, am I prepared to properly adore Him, Christ *my* Lord!

"It is good to praise the LORD and make music to your name, O most High" (Psalm 92:1).

LORD,

Thank you for meeting me on my level. Help me to grow in my understanding of the miraculous incarnation.

ACTIVITIES

Week 1

Mom

Within your city is someone special to you who doesn't know Jesus. Write her name on a 3 x 5 card. Plan to visit her one day this week. Write the day on your card and put the card where you will see it frequently. Every time you see the card thank God for creating such a neat person and ask Him for the words and opportunity to share His love with her when you visit.

Buy or make a small gift for her. You have prepared for this visit in prayer, so go with the confidence that God will use your words. Tell her you have been thanking God for her and use the Christmas season as a way to tell her about God's love for her.

Mom & Me

Tools: construction paper, crayons or markers, glue or tape, old newspapers, magazines, Christmas cards, or wrapping paper

Advance preparation: On the construction paper draw boxes and circles (totaling 25). Number the spaces. (See sample on page 155.)

1. Have your children color the page around the spaces and write this month's memory verse at the bottom of the page.
2. On December 1 put a picture of something you are thankful for in space 1 (e.g., home Bible, Jesus, friend, parents, pets, house, clothes, toys, trees, grandparents, food, clothes, flowers). Continue doing this for the next twenty-four days of the month. You may draw and color the pictures or cut them from Christmas cards, wrapping paper, magazines, or newspapers.
3. Review the memory verse, update your prayer list, and pray together. Thank God for all of the special things He gives us, but especially for His Son, Jesus.

JOHN 3:16

*For God so loved the world that he
gave his one and only Son, that
whoever believes in him shall not
perish but have eternal life.*

PRAY *EVERY* DAY

1.
2.
3.
4.

SUNDAY

MONDAY

TUESDAY

WEDNESDAY

THURSDAY

FRIDAY

SATURDAY

ACTIVITIES

Week 2

Mom

On a new 3 x 5 card, write the name of a special friend. List all the qualities your friend has that make her special to you and add to the list as you think of more things during the week. Put the card in a prominent place and thank God for your friend whenever you see it. Near the end of the week, using the information on the card, write a letter to your friend and tell her you have been thanking God for her. If she doesn't know the Lord, use this letter to tell her of God's love as well as yours. I can't think of a better Christmas present!

Mom & Me

Tools: a gift for each child (if you are caught in the holiday rush and don't have time to shop for a special gift, tuck a dollar bill into an envelope).

1. Sit in a cozy place with your children and tell them you want them to listen very carefully as you talk to God about them. Fold your hands, close your eyes, and thank God for each of your children. Mention each child's unique and endearing qualities. Tell the Lord how pleased you are with the children He has given to you. Avoid making any requests for forgiveness or pleas for better behavior; stick to thanking God for your children.

2. Hug your children and give them their gifts. **Explain:** *Because you are my children and I love you very much, I enjoy giving you gifts. I would give you just about anything to make you happy and to keep you safe. Because we are God's children and He loves us very much, He gave His Son Jesus to us as a special gift. Because of Jesus we can be happy and safe, and one day He will take us to live with God.*

3. Review the memory verse, update your prayer list, and pray together. Thank God for the special gift He gave to us.

JOHN 3:16
For God so loved the world that he
gave his one and only Son, that
whoever believes in him shall not
perish but have eternal life.

PRAY *EVERY* **DAY**
1.
2.
3.
4.

SUNDAY

MONDAY

TUESDAY

WEDNESDAY

THURSDAY

FRIDAY

SATURDAY

ACTIVITIES

Week 3

Mom

On another 3 x 5 card list the reasons you are thankful for your local church and put the card in a prominent place. Whenever you see the card pray for your church and pastor and thank God for them. Toward the end of the week, bake a Christmas goodie and take it to your pastor. Tuck your "praise" card inside the package of goodies as an additional surprise.

Mom & Me

Tools: construction paper, glitter, glue, crayons, markers.

1. Read John 3:16 together.
2. Think of someone in your neighborhood who needs to know about Jesus.
3. Give your child lots of space and equipment to create a wonderful Christmas card for that person.
4. Write the words of John 3:16 inside the card.
5. Deliver the card together. The Christmas message is beautifully illustrated by a child's love.
6. Review the memory verse, update your prayer list, and pray together.

JOHN 3:16

For God so loved the world that he
gave his one and only Son, that
whoever believes in him shall not
perish but have eternal life.

PRAY *EVERY* **DAY**

1.
2.
3.
4.

SUNDAY

MONDAY

TUESDAY

WEDNESDAY

THURSDAY

FRIDAY

SATURDAY

 **ACTIVITIES**

Week 4

Mom

Write JESUS on a new 3 x 5 card. As you thank God for His Son this week, list specific things that come to your mind about your relationship with Him. Rejoice this week as you recall God's goodness to you.

Mom & Me

1. Read Luke 2:1–20.
2. Suggested reading:

   God Cares When I'm Thankful, Elspeth Campbell Murphy, Chariot Books

   It's My Birthday, God, Elspeth Campbell Murphy, Chariot Books

   The Rumpoles and the Barleys, Karen Mezek, Harvest House
3. Review the memory verse, update your prayer list, and pray together.

JOHN 3:16

For God so loved the world that he gave his one and only Son, that whoever believes in him shall not perish but have eternal life.

PRAY *EVERY* DAY

1.
2.
3.
4.

SUNDAY

MONDAY

TUESDAY

WEDNESDAY

THURSDAY

FRIDAY

SATURDAY

SAMPLE ACTIVITY PAGES

 **JANUARY**

Learning God's Word

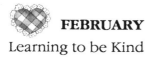 **FEBRUARY**

Learning to be Kind

MARCH

Learning to be Patient

APRIL
Learning to Forgive

MAY
Learning to Praise

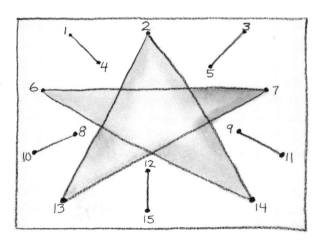

JUNE
Following God's Directions

 **JULY**
Trusting God's Promises

 **AUGUST**
Watching Our Words

SEPTEMBER
Seeing God's Miracles

OCTOBER

Lending a Hand

NOVEMBER

Spreading God's Love

DECEMBER

Giving Thanks to God

January, week 2, continued

5. Review the memory verse, update your prayer list, and pray together. Each day you say the verse put a picture or a sticker on the calendar.

February, week 1, continued

(Remind your child of safety rules concerning people she doesn't know. Tell her you want to go along if she decides to talk to someone new.)

5. Review the memory verse, update your prayer list, and pray together.

March, week 2, continued

5. Wiggle the roll like something is trying to come out. **Say:** *Little by little the caterpillar comes out from the sleeping bag, and see what God has made of him.* Break through the paper on the end of the roll and pull out the hidden butterfly.

6. **Explain:** *When we are patient and do what God tells us to do without losing our tempers or giving up, God will make something beautiful in our lives too.*

7. Review the memory verse, update your prayer list, and pray together.

April, week 2, continued

10. When she realizes you cannot, **say:** *That's right, we need Jesus to forgive our sins and clean up our lives.*

11. Pretend that the liquid dish detergent is God's forgiveness.

12. **Explain:** *When we go to God and tell Him we're sorry for the sins that are messing up our hearts, He always forgives us ... like this!*

13. Touch the tip of the toothpick to the soap so that a little soap is on the tip. Touch the tip to the middle of the water and watch what happens.
14. **Explain:** *When God forgives us, our sin goes away. The Bible says that it is gone, and God remembers it no more! Look into the water again. Can you see God's will more clearly? When sin is out of the way we can understand better what God wants us to do.*
15. Review the memory verse, update your prayer list, and pray together.

June, week 1, continued

5. Color it to make it pretty.
6. Discuss the importance of following directions.
7. Review the memory verse, update your prayer list, and pray together. Emphasize obedience.

June, week 2, continued

ter, 6 T. white sugar and 6 T. brown sugar (packed). Stir in 1/2 t. vanilla and 1 egg. Mix in contents of small bowl. Add 1 cup chocolate chips. Drop onto cookie sheet with a teaspoon and bake 9–11 minutes. Makes about 2 1/2 dozen cookies.
5. Review the memory verse, update your prayer list, and pray together.

(You may want to make something other than cookies. Choose a project that requires you to follow directions, such as a model airplane or a simple sewing project. I chose chocolate chip cookies because they are easy and it doesn't take long before you have a finished product.)

October, week 2, continued

     f. You and your sister want to watch different cartoon shows on different channels at the same time.

4. Review the memory verse, update your prayer list, and pray together.

November, week 2, continued

The world needs people who spread God's love just the way our lemonade needs sugar. Without salt, the world just isn't right!

5. Review the memory verse, update your prayer list, and pray together.